KidCaps' Presents

The War in Afganistan
A History Just for Kids

 **BOOKCAPS**

KidCaps is An Imprint of BookCaps™
www.bookcaps.com

© 2013. All Rights Reserved.

Table of Contents

About KidCaps

KidCaps is an imprint of BookCaps™ that is just for kids! Each month BookCaps will be releasing several books in this exciting imprint. Visit are website or like us on Facebook to see more!

Soldiers fight against Taliban soldiers in Afghanistan[1]

[1] Image source: http://rootsaction.org/

Introduction

Sergeant Mikey Hooper has never experienced heat like this before. Everything is wet and sticky: his socks, his undershirt, and even his underwear. The 115 degree weather makes him feel like he is inside of an oven, and the pack that he has to carry weighs over 80 pounds. Between the heat and the weight of his equipment (including the body armor that he wears under his vest) Mikey feels like he is moving in slow motion whenever he marches with his squad on patrol or when he is running towards an enemy's position. Basic training back in South Carolina had been intense, and at the time Mikey had thought that the Drill Instructors were just being mean by making the men run so much in the heat and go long periods without food and sleep. But now that he was here in Afghanistan, Mikey saw that the boot camp was meant to prepare him for the life of a Marine.

Sometimes he was woken up during the night by explosions, and sometimes he felt that he didn't always have enough water out here in the hot desert. When the combat finally started, though, he wasn't normally too scared. His months of experience had taught him to just stay focused on making sure that his men carried out their mission safely. Sometimes they had to protect Afghan civilians from the Taliban fighters; sometimes they had to enter caves and villages looking for the bad guys; sometimes they had to defend their fellow American and British soldiers from the attacks of Al-Qaeda fighters.

Today, Mikey and his men were in the mountains that lie to the east of the Afghan capital of Kabul. The area that they were walking in had been hit previously by American bombs, and now the soldiers were moving in, looking through the rubble and collapsed buildings for members of the Al-Qaeda terrorist organization, which was supported by the local Taliban government. As they walked between two high, rock hills, and around a bend in the road that led to the village, Mikey suddenly heard a distant *pop* and felt a pain that he could only describe as if somebody had punched him in the chest. He fell onto his back and used what little breath he had to warn his men about the attack.

A strong pair of hands grabbed him by the shoulders and pulled him back around the corner, behind the rocks that seemed to be exploding around him. The medic came running to look at him, but after catching his breath Mikey said "It hit my armor…I'm okay. Is anyone else hit?"

No one else was. Mikey had narrowly avoided getting killed by an Al-Qaeda sniper. The shots kept ringing out and echoing through the narrow canyon, and all the dust was making it hard to see what was going on. Mikey told his Corporal, John Eckard, to radio for an airstrike. While he did so, Mikey sat up and felt the blood rush to his head. With the help of the medic, he got to his feet and made a plan: they had to keep the Al-Qaeda fighters busy so that they wouldn't run away before the airstrike came in.

It was decided that they would split into two groups. One would stay back and provide cover fire while Mikey and the other half moved forward and engaged the enemy. Within thirty seconds, the plan was underway. While the men in the back fired small bursts of fire with their guns, Mikey and his men moved in pairs around the corner and behind some large rocks twenty yards ahead. The canyon was alive with the sounds of yelling and small explosions. It seemed like the enemy didn't have any grenades or rockets, which was a good thing for Mikey and his men; they wouldn't have been able to escape the explosion of shrapnel. Even so, those bullets were still plenty scary when they came flying towards your head.

For ten minutes, the fighting got more and more intense. Mikey could hardly stick his helmet out from around the rock without pieces of it exploding in his face from all the enemy bullets. Finally, a message came over the radio that the plane was on its way. The Navy had sent two F/A-18 Hornets from a carrier stationed in the North Arabian Sea. The pilots of the jets had requested that a smoke grenade be thrown to mark the men's position. Mikey gave the order and a grenade was thrown that signaled their position. Mikey grabbed the radio and said: "The target is east of the orange smoke, I repeat: east of the orange smoke." He clicked off the radio and yelled "Bombs away!"

His men all dropped to the ground and yelled "Bombs away!" The enemy must have figured out that something was happening when they saw the smoke because the bullets stopped flying and Mikey could just make out the shapes of men running away through the smoke and dust. Mikey assumed they were going to try to retreat to the other side of the hills, but it was too late for that. Mikey and his men had succeeded in giving the Navy boys perfect targets, a group of sitting ducks. The Marines never saw the jets; they just heard them for a split second before two massive explosions shook the entire canyon. By the time the smoke and dust had cleared, it was clear that there was no one was left to fire at them.

Even so, Mikey and his moved carefully towards the enemy's position seventy yards away. They found a mess of dead bodies. No one laughed or joked. They weren't happy to have helped to kill these men. But, these men were terrorists who wanted to hurt innocent people. They had refused to stop being violent, so they had to be stopped. It was that simple.

Mikey grabbed the radio from the soldier who carried it. "This is Sergeant Hooper confirming 16 hostiles down, no casualties among my men." The voice on the other end congratulated him for completing his mission without losing a single man. Mikey said thanks and sat down with his back against the rocky wall. Taking a drink of water, he felt himself getting dizzy, forgetting that just a few minutes earlier he had been shot in the chest. The medic saw him and recommended that they head back to base so that Mikey could get checked out.

Mikey smiled. *Base.* It made it sound like they were a bunch of kids out here playing hide-and-seek. He agreed with the medic, gave the order to move out, and headed back with his men towards the camp. Tomorrow would be another day, with another mission, and another tough decision to make. But none of that mattered right now. He had survived this battle; he had survived another day in Afghanistan.

Does it sound like it would be exciting to fight alongside the brave Marines in Afghanistan? While sometimes it sounds like something out of a movie, the reality of war is different. There aren't actually a lot of heroes like the ones we see in theaters; more than anything you see teams of people working together and just trying to survive another day. The soldiers who kill their enemies aren't always happy about what they've done; they just see it as something that they have been told to do by their superiors, and they carry out the job. Even though it isn't quite over yet, the War in Afghanistan has had a big impact in the world. Do you know anyone who was involved in that war or who has an opinion about it?

In this book, we will learn a lot about the War in Afghanistan. The first section will tell us more about what led up to it. We will look a little at the history of Afghanistan to find out how such bad guys like the Taliban could ever become the ruling party in the country. We will also see a little of what life was like when the Taliban was in charge.

Then, in the next section, we will see why the war actually happened. Although things had been bad in Afghanistan for a while, why did the United Nations decide to get involved in 2001? The answer had a lot to do with the terrorist attack of September 11, 2001, and with a lot of strong emotions. We will also see in this section that some people think that the war was and still is illegal, and that no one should have fought it.

Then, we will see some of the interesting details of how the war was fought. The beginning was pretty standard, but the final part has been difficult and the NATO (North Atlantic Treaty Organization) troops are still having a tough time doing their job and keeping the region stable and safe. Along with the bravery of the NATO troops, we will also see how many Afghan men and women have been affected by the war and how they have helped to fight against the bad guys.

The section after that will show us what it would be like to be a kid living in Afghanistan during the war. Daily life was changed in many ways from before the war; sometimes in a good way and sometimes in a bad way. Then, the next sections will talk about how the war started to wind down and what significant changes Afghanistan has seen since it started.

Are you ready to learn more about this war? As we do so, try to keep an eye out for how the religion of the Taliban and Al-Qaeda fighters has affected their actions and the way that they deal with outside nations. Whether or not anyone meant for it to, religion became a central factor in this war and continues to be so in everything that happens in Afghanistan today. So buckle up, and let's move on to the next section!

Chapter 1: What Led Up to the War in Afghanistan?

Afghanistan is a country with a rich history[2]

The country that we now know as Afghanistan used to be under the influence of the British Empire. For several decades, the Afghan people had to listen to the British and make decisions that would make them happy. Eventually, the Afghan people became independent of the British, and some of their leaders tried hard to make their country a better place. But no matter how hard they tried, those leaders could never make everyone happy at the same time. No matter

---

[2] Image source: http://travel.nationalgeographic.com/

who was in charge, it seemed like someone else had a better idea of how to do things and how the Afghan people should live their lives. This led to a lot of violence throughout the years, and even some periods of absolute civil war.

During World War Two and the Cold War, Afghanistan stayed neutral, which means that they didn't take one side or the other. They decided to just worry about their own problems and not those of other countries. But in 1978, Afghan people who liked the Communist way of doing things overthrew the local government to try and make a government like the one that the U.S.S.R. (the Soviets) had.

As you can imagine, not everyone was happy about it. Those who didn't like Communism started to fight back and thus a civil war began. The Soviets got involved to help their fellow party members and soon there were Soviet soldiers marching in the streets and mountaintops of Afghanistan as part of the war also. The United States thought that the Soviets were trying to spread their influence and started to get scared and for a while it looked like the U.S. might even get involved in the fighting too. Although they didn't send any soldiers, they did send money and weapons to help the anti-communist fighters, and it wasn't until 1989 when the Soviets finally left.

From 1989 to 1992, the anti-communist fighters (called the Mujahedeen) who had fought against the Soviets now turned their attention to the Afghan Communists. The Mujahedeen were supported by the

U.S., and they were finally able to overthrow the Communist government in 1992, after three years of fighting. In case you are counting, you are probably starting to realize that since at least 1978 this area has had one war after another for many years. The one that started in 1978 when the Communists took over was called the Saur Revolution, and marked the time when the common people started to fight against the government.

As we saw, in 1992, the Communist government was overthrown, and on April 24 the different political groups got together to decide how to run the country now that the Communists weren't in charge anymore. They formed something called the "Peshawar Accord". All of the groups (but one) agreed to form a new country called The Islamic State of Afghanistan. They thought that they had found a new way to run the country without outside interference and without fighting anymore. However, one political party, named Hezbi Islami, did not agree. With help from Pakistan, they began to attack their fellow Afghanis and to try to prevent any efforts at peace and unity.

Some other nearby countries liked what was going on in Afghanistan and so didn't try to stop the fighting. They thought that if Afghanistan fell apart then they could take over the land and make their own countries stronger. So Saudi Arabia and Iran each supported other groups within the Afghan government, playing them like chess pieces, hoping that eventually the country would be too weak to defend itself and that an outside country could just move in and become the new boss.

As you can imagine, it wasn't a great time to be living in Afghanistan. There were different groups if people fighting for control of the country and the groups all seemed to be hurting lots of people and getting away with it. There was the main government in the capital that was under attack by Hezbi Islami, and then other parts of the country were under control of local militias (small armies) who got their money from foreign countries. Many of the common people felt like no one was looking out for them and that no one had their interests in mind. Thousands of Afghanis had run away to other countries, and those who stayed sometimes had to worry about being attacked by the militia groups. Who would protect them?

In Pakistan, young Afghan Muslim refugees had gone to special religious schools where they were taught about a variety of subjects. Those who went to these schools would sometimes go back to their country and stick together in groups, to protect each other against the bad conditions. One young man, named Mohammed Omar, had gone to one of these schools and was tired of seeing his fellow Afghans mistreated by the militias and of seeing so many people not respecting his religion of Islam. Together with a group of about 50 friends, he formed a new political and religious group called the Taliban in his hometown of Kandahar, near the border with Pakistan.

The Taliban quickly earned the reputation of being people who enforce the laws of the Islamic holy book, the Quran. In the spring of 1994, they were reported to have freed two girls who had been kidnapped and mistreated by a local militia. They punished the people responsible, and the local citizens were happy that someone was looking out for them, someone who believed and respected the same things as they did.

Within a few months, thousands of young men joined this exciting new group, and they started to fight to take over Afghanistan and to unify it under one type of rule, a type of government that respected the religion of Islam above all else. During 1994, they took over about one-third of Afghanistan's provinces and the people living there. In early 1995, they began to attack the capital city of Kabul. But things weren't so easy, and the Taliban started to lose a lot of battles against the main government of Afghanistan.

Finally, on September 27, 1996, the Taliban moved into the capital (which the main government had abandoned so as not to be fighting in the city streets) and established themselves as the new bosses. While some people thought that the Taliban were honestly just like a big puppet for Pakistan, others were happy to see leaders who took their jobs seriously and who wanted to make the Islamic religion a part of the government and everyday life of the people.

Once they were in the capital, the Taliban wanted to make sure they were in control in the whole country. To do so, they used violence. During the next few years, from 1996 to 2001, reports started to come out of mean things done to people who broke the laws of the Taliban or who refused to support them. Some people were beat, and others were even killed. We will see more in a future section about some of the bad things that the Taliban is accused of having done.

The Taliban, along with treating its own people harshly, also started to get a bad reputation because of the friends that they had; in particular, for having connections with Al-Qaeda, a terrorist organization founded by Osama Bin Laden. This friendship would soon make the enemies of Al-Qaeda the enemies of Afghanistan.

Chapter 2: Why Did the War in Afghanistan Happen?

As we have seen, things in Afghanistan weren't going terrifically well. The Afghan people hadn't had a stable government for a long time, and the people who were in charge weren't always the nicest guys. The country was finally taken over by a new religious and political group called the Taliban, but they seemed to do as much bad stuff as they did good stuff. So you might wonder why anyone from another country would get involved. The Afghan people might not react well to a foreign government marching in, and the Taliban certainly would not be happy about it. So why did the United States (together with several other countries) lead an invasion into this country?

The world knew what was happening in Afghanistan, but it seemed more like something that Afghanistan itself and their neighbors should be worried about. Why should the United States and other Western countries worry about what was happening on the other side of the globe?

All of that changed on September 11, 2001.

The World Trade Center burns after the September 11, 2001 terrorist attack[3]

Do you remember hearing about the terrorist attacks of September 11, 2001? Four planes from the east coast were stolen by a group of nineteen terrorists. They hijacked the planes once they were in the air and made the planes fly in a different direction. Two of them were flown into the World Trade Centers; one was flown into the Pentagon building in Washington D.C.; and one crashed in Pennsylvania, perhaps on its way to Washington D.C.

The United States and honestly the whole world were stunned and absolutely surprised by the attacks. Although it was not the first time that terrorists had attacked the United States, or even the World Trade Center itself, it was the first time that anyone had

[3] Image source: http://commons.wikimedia.org/

been so successful and that so many people had died. 2,977 people were killed in the attacks, plus the 19 hijackers. Others died later on because of sickness or injuries received during the rescue attempts.

The world watched on live TV as the buildings fell, as desperate people trapped in the burning towers jumped to their deaths, and as firefighters tried their best to save the victims. Americans were glued to their TVs for hours and cried as they saw the horrible scenes happen live and then again as they were replayed over and over again. Even for people living in faraway California and Hawaii, it felt like the terrorists were in their backyard.

The American people had been hit hard by terrorism, and lots of families had suffered for it. The American people wanted revenge. They wanted to find the people responsible and to make them pay. Even though the hijackers themselves were dead, they wanted to find the people that had taught, trained, and sent the hijackers on this mission of death. But how could they ever identify the hijackers? Like an exciting movie, the clues started to come together in the hours and days following the attacks. Within 72 hours, all of the hijackers had been identified. How?

Knowing that they were going to die during the attacks, the hijackers left behind a lot of clues and did not try to hide who they were. They bought their tickets with their credit cards, used their real names when making the room reservations, and left clues in hotel rooms and parked cars that were soon discovered. It was learned that the 19 attackers were religious fanatics from the Islam religion. Do you know what a fanatic is? A religious fanatic is someone who goes to extremes for their faith and is willing to hurt other people if they don't have the same religion as them. These men were Islamic fanatics and believed that the attacks were a part of a *jihad*, or holy Islamic war.

Can you believe that? The men who killed so many innocent victims, including kids, thought that God would reward them for their actions. But who trained and prepared these 19 fanatics to do this terrible thing, to carry out the attacks of September 11th? It was learned that all 19 of the men were members of an organization called Al-Qaeda, a terrorist group started by a man named Osama Bin Laden.

Now the American people wanted to find Osama Bin Laden and rest of his Al-Qaeda group and make them pay for what they had done. On September 18, 2001, a special law was passed that gave the President permission to use military authority in order to find and stop the terrorists responsible for the attacks. But where was Al-Qaeda hiding? It was learned that they were in camps and caves spread across Afghanistan.

How did the President of the United States, George W. Bush, think that Americans could get a hold of those terrorists living so far away? In a statement to Congress on September 20, 2001, he made the position of the United States clear, and he also made a demand of the Taliban government in Afghanistan.

During that speech, he said important some pretty important things about Al-Qaeda and their relationship to the Taliban. For example, look at the quote below:

> "The leadership of al Qaeda has great influence in Afghanistan and supports the Taliban regime in controlling most of that country. In Afghanistan, we see al Qaeda's vision for the world.
> Afghanistan's people have been brutalized -- many are starving, and many have fled. Women are not allowed to attend school. You can be jailed for owning a television. Religion can be practiced only as their leaders dictate. A man can be jailed in Afghanistan if his beard is not long enough.
>
> The United States respects the people of Afghanistan -- after all, we are currently its largest source of humanitarian aid -- but we condemn the Taliban regime. It is not only repressing its own people, it is threatening people everywhere by sponsoring and sheltering and supplying terrorists. By aiding and abetting murder, the Taliban regime is committing murder."[4]

During this speech, given just nine days after the attacks of September 11th, President Bush makes it clear that the Taliban is best friends with Al-Qaeda and that the Taliban is a dangerous government guilty

[4] Quptation source: http://georgewbush-whitehouse.archives.gov/

of doing some awful things to its people. In his speech, President Bush continued:

> "And tonight, the United States of America makes the following demands on the Taliban: Deliver to United States authorities all the leaders of al Qaeda who hide in your land. Release all foreign nationals, including American citizens, you have unjustly imprisoned. Protect foreign journalists, diplomats and aid workers in your country. Close immediately and permanently every terrorist training camp in Afghanistan, and hand over every terrorist, and every person in their support structure, to appropriate authorities. Give the United States full access to terrorist training camps, so we can make sure they are no longer operating. Our enemy is a radical network of terrorists, and every government that supports them. These demands are not open to negotiation or discussion. The Taliban must act, and act immediately. They will hand over the terrorists, or they will share in their fate. From this day forward, any nation that continues to harbor or support terrorism will be regarded by the United States as a hostile regime."[5]

---

[5] Quotation source: http://georgewbush-whitehouse.archives.gov/

President Bush during his September 20, 2001 speech to Congress[6]

Do you understand how important those words were? President Bush was essentially telling the Taliban that if they didn't hand over Al-Qaeda and shut down the camps, then the United States was going to fight against them the same as they were fighting against Al-Qaeda! The American people wanted to stop the terrorists responsible for the 9/11 attacks, and this was the best way that they knew how.

Along with the fact that the Taliban was protecting the Al-Qaeda terrorists, President Bush also mentioned how bad life was under the Taliban rule. He mentioned how severe punishments were given

[6] Image source: http://www.historycommons.org/

for something like not having a long beard or for owning a television. So the United States and other countries were also worried about the human rights abuses happening in the country. Do you know what "human rights" means? It means the right that all people have to a certain amount of freedom and to not have to worry about certain things. For example, no one should have to worry about whether the government will hurt them, whether the police will do the right thing, or whether they will have enough food to eat; those are basic human rights. However, in Afghanistan, when the Taliban was in charge, not everyone had those rights. Some people were mistreated by the police, others didn't have enough food, and others weren't even allowed to leave the house.

Women, especially, were not given a lot of freedom under Taliban rule; a lot of girls weren't allowed to go to school or even to leave the house unless they were accompanied by a man. Would you like to have lived in a country like that?

So how did the Taliban respond to President Bush's demand that they hand over the leaders of Al-Qaeda? The Taliban did not want to cooperate with the United States. Not only did it view them as a foreign power that shouldn't be pushing them around but it also thought that because the American government wasn't organized according to the teachings of Islam that it wouldn't handle the situation properly. So, the Taliban refused to turn over Al-Qaeda and Osama Bin laden and instead suggested on October 5, 2001 that if the U.S. could provide enough proof then the Taliban would try Bin Laden in an Afghan court.

That answer wasn't good enough for President Bush. On October 7, 2001, United States Special Forces entered the country and at the same time the bombing of the capital started. The War in Afghanistan had begun.

Chapter 3: What Happened During the War in Afghanistan?

When the United States invaded Afghanistan on October 7, 2001 in an operation called "Operation Enduring Freedom. The operation had two main goals:

- find and capture all members of Al-Qaeda and bring them to justice
- put an end to and replace the Taliban regime that mistreated the Afghan people

In order to meet these goals, it was decided to start with a bombing campaign like normal but also to quickly move in troops to start taking over the villages and provinces of Afghanistan. The bombing began that same day as the invasion and made it easier for troops to take over important military positions. Planes from way up high in the sky dropped bombs on Al-Qaeda training camps, and Apache helicopters attacked special targets and were strong enough to not be shot down by the Taliban's anti-aircraft guns.

An Apache helicopter used by the British during the War in Afghanistan[7]

Something else that President Bush said during his speech on September 20 made a lot of people start thinking. He said:

> "Perhaps the NATO Charter reflects best the attitude of the world: An attack on one is an attack on all. The civilized world is rallying to America's side. They understand that if this terror goes unpunished, their own cities, their own citizens may be next. Terror, unanswered, can not only bring down buildings, it can threaten the stability of legitimate governments. And you know what -- we're not going to allow it."[8]

---

[7] Image source: http://www.marinecorpstimes.com/

[8] Quotation source: http://georgewbush-whitehouse.archives.gov/

In his speech, President Bush tried to explain that Americans weren't the only ones who should be worried about the activities of Al-Qaeda and the Taliban. He made it clear that an attack against one Western nation was like an attack against all of them, because they were all partners and because they all stood for the same thing. For that reason, some countries chose to help the United States with the invasion, including Great Britain, Australia, and Canada. But how did the Taliban and Al-Qaeda respond to the invasion?

Of course, the Taliban and Al-Qaeda used all of their weapons and energy to fight against the invading forces, called "The Coalition". The Taliban, because it was identified mainly by its religious beliefs and practices, felt like it was being targeted because of its faith, and not its politics. They went so far as to say that what the United States and Coalition were doing was an "attack on Islam."

In November of 2002, Osama Bin laden gave an interview where he threatened all Western nations that attacked any Islamic nation. He said:

> "What do your governments want by allying themselves with the criminal gang in the White House against Muslims? What do your governments want from their alliance with America in attacking us in Afghanistan? I mention in particular Britain, France, Italy, Canada, Germany and Australia. We warned Australia before not to join in [the war] in

Afghanistan, and [against] its despicable effort to separate East Timor. It ignored the warning until it woke up to the sounds of explosions in Bali…This is unfair. It is time that we get even. You will be killed just as you kill, and will be bombed just as you bomb."[9]

Yes, both the Taliban and Al-Qaeda saw the War in Afghanistan as part of something larger. Instead of seeing it as punishment for the attacks of 9/11 or for their harsh treatment of the people of Afghanistan, they felt like they were the victims. They felt like they were being attacked for their faith and that any fighting that they did, any further terrorist attacks, would be to defend themselves and their way of life. Do you agree with them or do you think that they were missing the point?

The initial fighting was over by early December, when the last city was taken over by the Coalition forces. The Taliban had dispersed into the general population without surrendering. Al-Qaeda was chased into the mountains, and many members were forced to run away from Afghanistan into nearby Pakistan. On December 7, 2004, Hamid Karzai was voted to be the first democratically elected President of Afghanistan, a position which he still holds today. It looked like things were going well.

---

[9] Quotation source: http://news.bbc.co.uk/

The first democratically elected President of Afghanistan, Hamid Karzai[10]

But then, in 2006, things started to get complicated again. The Taliban began to get back together and started to fight back against the Coalition forces, made up primarily of Afghan, American, and British soldiers. The war became a type of Guerilla warfare where the fighting happened in the streets of the cities and in the distant mountains and caves. The soldiers had to be on the lookout constantly to make sure that no enemies were shooting at them from abandoned buildings and villages. Sometimes, they look for something called a "combat indicator", which were

[10] Image source: http://www.twitched-reality.com/

signs that a fight was about to happen. Sometimes that meant groups of people running away from a certain area when they saw Taliban and Coalition soldiers marching towards each other.

Villagers run away from a village full of Taliban soldiers, a sign that there is about to be fighting[11]

The troops have learned to be prepared for sneak attacks and have helped to train the local Afghan military and police to take over in fighting against the Taliban. Even so, it is not a rare thing to hear in the news about Americans dying in Afghanistan due to car bombs Taliban attacks, or helicopter accidents. It is still a dangerous place to be.

---

[11] Image source: http://www.youtube.com/

Chapter 4: What Was It Like to Be a Kid During the War in Afghanistan?

Can you imagine what it would have been like to be a kid living in Afghanistan during all of these events? First off, you would have been genuinely worried about your family when the Taliban was in charge. Do you remember some of the bad things that they did to other people when they were the bosses?

One of the worst things was the way that women were treated. Young girls didn't always get to go to school, and grown women couldn't leave the house unless they were accompanied by a man. Also, many of the women had to thoroughly cover themselves, and if they showed their faces in public they were punished by being beaten with a stick.

The Taliban had a specific way on understanding the Islamic religion, and as President Bush said, if you disobeyed the rules that they made you might get killed. Would you have liked to have lived in a government like that? Of course not! No one wants to have their freedom of choice taken away!

But the problems didn't end when the United States and Coalition forces moved in. Instead of living under an oppressive government, kids now had to see what it was like to live in a war zone. They had to worry about bullets coming through the walls and bombing being dropped on nearby buildings. They had to see people from faraway lands marching down their streets and sometimes they had to run away from their houses and villages with nothing but the clothes in their backs. During the War in Afghanistan, millions of people left the country because it was just plain too dangerous to live there.

Two Afghan children flee their village from the Taliban fighters that took it over[12]

What would you have thought about the War in Afghanistan if you were a kid living there? Well, you might be like Osama Bin Laden who thought that the Americans and others were attacking your religion, or you might be like many other Afghan people who were happy to have someone from the outside come in and make their country more stable and to help it take steps to have a better government.

---

[12] Image source: http://www.youtube.com/

Chapter 5: How Did the War in Afghanistan End?

In this section, we can't actually talk about how the War in Afghanistan ended, because the fighting is still going on. However, we can talk about how the fighting has changed and how it is coming to an end/ We can also talk about what plans the Coalition and Afghan governments have in order to bring an end to foreign action in the area.

Although Presidents Bush and Obama have thought that it was necessary to send in more troops at different times throughout the war, in recent months there has been talk about "troop withdrawal". The Presidents of the United States and Afghanistan, along with the Prime Minister of Great Britain, have the final goal of making sure that Afghanistan is a strong and independent nation that won't fall under the control of extremists like the Taliban ever again.

In order to make that happen, the Coalition forces decided to give the new Afghan government control of the country piece by piece. Starting in the spring of 2013, control over all prisons and prisoners was to be given over to the Afghan people. By the end of 2014, the handover will be complete and all Coalition troops (who have been under the control of NATO since 2003) will be able to go home, their mission accomplished.

In the meantime, President Karzai has tried to make contact with Taliban leaders living in Pakistan and other areas to try and make peace with them, but his efforts haven't been successful. But the lower amount of fighting and improved laws have helped millions of Afghan people living in other countries to come home and start to repair the economy and other parts of the country.

The Afghan people are learning how to work together to make their country better, and knowing that, by 2014, there will be no more NATO troops, they are taking steps to be prepared to keep fighting against the Taliban and other people who want to make the country a worse place. In fact, there are now female soldiers working side by side with male soldiers, and they are helping to find and identify Taliban fighters hiding in houses and neighborhoods. Their work makes the cities in Afghanistan safer for everyone involved.

Individual villages are getting together small groups of soldiers who are ready to fight the Taliban if they should ever come back. One man, named Safer Mohammad, spoke about trying to stop some members of the Taliban from taking away his son. He told the story of how it happened:

> "Four men pushed me to the ground and started beating me. At this moment my other son came out of the house and started firing at them. We had an old rifle from the time of the

jihad and we managed to chase off eight Taliban with it…They demanded food, money and accommodation, and they brought nothing good for the residents. Now these have made up their minds: they will not shelter them again or even allow them in the area."[13]

Safer Mohammed and his family fought back against the Taliban[14]

The Taliban and even Al-Qaeda no longer have a strong influence over the people of Afghanistan, and although they may try to do bad things to their enemies, they are constantly being chased down by the good guys and are having a hard time carrying out their plans. As the story of Safer Mohammed shows, the Afghan people are not willing to be bossed around by bad leaders anymore.

[13] Quotation source: http://www.afghanistan-today.org/

[14] Image source: http://www.afghanistan-today.org/

The War in Afghanistan is almost over, and it looks like it has been successful.

Chapter 6: What Happened After the War in Afghanistan?

Although there is still some fighting going on, things truly have changed since the Taliban was in charge and the U.S.-led Coalition invaded Afghanistan in 2001. While not everything is perfect, some important steps have been taken towards important goals. Like what?

The first has to do with the improved conditions of several groups within the country. Before, women were mistreated, but now they have much more freedom than before. As we saw, some of them have even started to fight alongside male Afghans to protect their country from the Taliban! Also, many young girls now have the opportunity to go to school. Before the 2001 invasion, only 50,000 girls in the *whole* country were going to school, but today there are almost three million girls going to school! Isn't that great!

Also, although the economy is not as great as it could be, there aren't people starving in the streets like before. Due to a combination of charity and hard work from the Afghan people themselves, the country is starting to take care of the needs of its entire people.

Afghanistan is recovering from all the damage after years of war[15]

Of course, that's not to say that everything has been super smooth and problem free. In February of 2012, some U.S. soldiers on a military base in Afghanistan accidentally burnt some copies of the Islamic holy book, called the Quran. They thought that they were burning terrorist literature with secret messages on it, but by the time they realized their mistake it was too late. The burning of the holy book by people of a different faith was too much for some Afghan people and in protests outside the base thousands of angry men shouted and told the Americans to go home. Even though it didn't lead to anything major, it

---

[15] Image source: http://www.fotopedia.com/

showed how quickly a misunderstanding can affect thousands of people.

As the War in Afghanistan winds down, some in the United States and other places have started to wonder if it was the right thing to do in the first place. Some feel that the United States rushed into the war because it was angry about the attacks of 9/11 and that the war itself was actually illegal. Is that the case?

Most of the people who criticize the War in Afghanistan say that President Bush and the other Coalition countries never had the legal authority to attack another nation. Why not? Well, all of the countries (including Afghanistan) are part of the United Nations and have agreed to live by its laws. Among them is Article 51 of the U.N. Charter, which says:

> "Nothing in the present Charter shall impair the inherent right of individual or collective self-defence if an armed attack occurs against a Member of the United Nations, until the Security Council has taken measures necessary to maintain international peace and security. Measures taken by Members in the exercise of this right of self-defence shall be immediately reported to the Security Council and shall not in any way affect the authority and responsibility of the Security Council under the present Charter to take at any time such action as it deems necessary in order to

maintain or restore international peace and security."[16]

In other words, even though a country is part of the United Nations, they can always defend themselves if attacked by someone else. The Coalition forces, in particular the United States, felt that they were allowed to fight against Afghanistan because Afghanistan was helping Al-Qaeda, the ones who had attacked American on 9/11. However, other people still think that because it wasn't the *government* of Afghanistan that ordered the attacks then the war was illegal and should never have happened.

Although it is too late to change anything or to undo all of the damage done by the war; what do you think? Was it right of the U.S. to invade Afghanistan to stop the Taliban and Al-Qaeda or should they have found a different way to solve the problem?

---

[16] Quotation source: http://www.un.org/

Conclusion

The War in Afghanistan was a important time in the history of everyone involved. Thousands of people died, entire governments were replaced, and justice was served on some men who had done some bad things. Did you learn something new from this manual? Let's review some of the most important points.

The first section told us more about what led up to the fighting. We looked a little at the history of Afghanistan to find out how such bad guys like the Taliban could ever become the ruling party in the country. Do you remember how when the Taliban first arrived it looked like they were going to help the people? How disappointed many Afghans must have felt when they realized that the Taliban were just going to hurt them and take advantage of them like so many others had before.

Then, in the next section, we saw why the war itself actually happened. Although things had been bad in Afghanistan for a while, why did the United Nations decide to get involved in 2001? The answer had a lot to do with the terrorist attack of September 11, 2001, and with a lot of strong emotions. After the World Trade Center and other targets were attacked, the American people wanted to bring to justice anyone who had been involved in the planning of the attacks. Once they found out that Al-Qaeda was the group that had organized everything, they were determined to make sure that the members of Al-Qaeda paid for their crimes.

Even though Al-Qaeda was being protected by another country (Afghanistan) President Bush made it clear that anyone who helped the bad guys was like a bad guy himself. So because the Taliban helped Al-Qaeda and protected them from punishment, the Coalition felt that the Taliban had to go too.

Then, we saw some of the interesting details of how the war was fought. The beginning was pretty standard, but the final part has been difficult and the NATO (North Atlantic Treaty Organization) troops are still having a tough time doing their job and keeping the region stable and safe. They have to fight small groups of soldiers who hide in the mountains and in villages, and the fighting never seems to stop. Along with the bravery of the NATO troops, we also saw how many Afghan men and women have been affected by the war and how they have helped to fight against the bad guys.

The section after that showed us what it would be like to be a kid living in Afghanistan during the war. Daily life was changed in many ways from before the war; sometimes in a good way and sometimes in a bad way. Little boys and girls get to go to school now, but some of them are still scared that they wil be hurt in the fighting and some of them are still quite poor.